BRITAIN IN OLD PHOTOGRAPHS

THE MANCHESTER REGIMENT

THE 63RD & 96TH REGIMENTS OF FOOT

ROBERT BONNER

First published 2011
Reprinted, 2019

The History Press
97 St George's Place, Cheltenham,
Gloucestershire, GL50 3QB
www.thehistorypress.co.uk

© Robert Bonner 2011

The right of Robert Bonner to be identified as the Author
of this work has been asserted in accordance with the
Copyrights, Designs and Patents Act 1988.

All rights reserved. No part of this book may be reprinted
or reproduced or utilised in any form or by any electronic,
mechanical or other means, now known or hereafter invented,
including photocopying and recording, or in any information
storage or retrieval system, without the permission in writing
from the Publishers.
British Library Cataloguing in Publication Data.
A catalogue record for this book is available from the British Library.

ISBN 978 0 7524 6015 4
Typesetting and origination by The History Press
Printed in Great Britain by TJ International Ltd, Padstow, Cornwall.

CONTENTS

	Military Abbreviations	4
	Introduction	5
1	Pre-1881	9
2	1881–1900	17
3	The Anglo-Boer War	29
4	1892–1914	41
5	The Great War, 1914–1918	51
6	Between the Wars, 1919–1939	63
7	The Second World War, 1939–1945	81
8	The Final Days, 1946–1958	97

MILITARY ABBREVIATIONS

ADC	Aide-de-Camp	Lt-Com.	Lieutenant-Commander
Adj.	Adjutant	Lt-Gen.	Lieutenant-General
Adj.-Gen.	Adjutant-General	2nd-Lt	Second Lieutenant
AVM	Air Vice Marshall	Maj.	Major
Bn (bn)	Battalion	Maj.-Gen.	Major-General
Capt.	Captain	MM	Military Medal
Capt. & Adj.	Captain & Adjuntant	NCO	Non-Commissioned Officer
Cdr	Commander	Pte	Private
Co.	Company	OCPD	Officer Commanding Police District
CO	Commanding Officer		
Col.-Sgt	Colour Sergeant	QM	Quartermaster
Cpl	Corporal	QMG	Quartermaster-General
CSM	Company Sergeant Major	QMS	Quartermaster-Sergeant
DCM	Distinguished Conduct Medal	RSM	Regimental Sergeant-Major
		Sgt	Sergeant
DFC	Distinguished Flying Cross	Sgt-Maj.	Sergeant-Major
DFM	Distinguished Flying Medal	S/Sgt	Staff-Sergeant
DSM	Distinguished Service Medal	Sqn Cdr	Squadron Commander
DSO	Distinguished Service Order	Sub-Lt	Sub-Lieutenant
Flg-Off	Flying Officer	WO	Warrant Officer
Gen.	General	LDV	Local Defence Volunteers (later Home Guard)
GCM	general court martial		
GOC	General Officer Commanding	LTA	Lighter-than-air
		MM	Military Medal
Gp Capt.	Group Captain	POW	prisoner of war
GSM	General Service Medal	Regt (regt)	regiment
Gy Sgt	Gunnery Sergeant	RFC	Royal Flying Corps
L/Cpl	Lance-Corporal	Sqn	Squadron
L/Sgt	Lance Sergeant	TA	Territorial Army
Lt	Lieutenant	VAD	Voluntary Aid Detachment
Lt-Col.	Lieutenant-Colonel	VC	Victoria Cross

INTRODUCTION

In 1756 the Holy Roman Empire, consisting of Austria, France, Russia, Sweden and Saxony, joined in a coalition to cripple or destroy Prussia. England, already involved in war with France in North America and India, supported Prussia. So began the Seven Years' War, bringing with it an expansion of the British Army by fifteen battalions, which were raised by forming second battalions to existing infantry of the line regiments. A second battalion was raised to the 8th Regiment of Foot or King's Regiment. On 21 April 1758, this second battalion of the 8th Foot was constituted a regiment in its own right and numbered 63rd.

The 63rd Regiment spent most of 1758 in the west of England. The earliest reference to the uniform of the time and the regimental colour is given in a Clothing Warrant dated November 1758, which stated that the coats were to have buff linings with very deep green facings. The drummers' coats were to be of the same shade of green with red facings. Later that year, the 63rd sailed as part of an expeditionary force to seize the French West Indies, taking part in the capture of the island of Guadeloupe, for which it received its first battle honour. The regiment's first Commanding Officer, Lt-Col. Peter Desbrisay, was killed in action at the citadel of Basse Terre. From this campaign the regiment later adopted as its badge the fleur-de-lys, the French national emblem. The 63rd remained in the West Indies until 1764 and probably considered itself lucky that it had only been five years – the 38th Foot had been left in the disease-ridden West Indies for nearly sixty years.

Reinforcements were sent to the war in America in 1775 and with them went the 63rd. They first saw action at the Battle of Bunker Hill. The Grenadier and Light Companies of the 63rd were actively engaged in this action. When the long, drawn-out war came to an end in 1782, the regiment was part of the garrison of Charleston. At the withdrawal of British troops in December 1782, the 63rd was sent to Jamaica. On 23 February 1783, whilst stationed in the West Indies, the regiment was given the title of 'the 63rd West Suffolk Regiment'.

From 1800 the 63rd led a wandering existence, joining a force which was intended to make various diversions against France in the Mediterranean. It helped garrison Turin, Minorca, Gibraltar and Malta until May 1803, when it sailed to Ireland and was stationed there until November 1807. In August 1804 a second battalion of the 63rd Regiment was raised, but only continued in existence until 1814, when it was disbanded. During its short life, it saw active service in the ill-fated and badly managed Walcheren expedition of 1808.

During the three years spent in Australia between 1829 and 1932, the 63rd had its headquarters in Hobart Town, Van Diemen's Land, with the rest of the regiment split into detachments varying in strength from seventy-one men from all ranks to just two private soldiers, amongst forty-seven different posts all over the colony. The 63rd, as a part of the allied armies in the Crimea, served there between 1854 and 1955. From there the 63rd went to Halifax, Nova Scotia, remaining in Canada until 1865. The second Afghan war broke out in 1877 and, following the disaster at Maiwand in southern Afghanistan, the 63rd was selected to take part in the second phase of the campaign when they occupied Kandahar. A year later they were back on the Afghan border, manning outposts in an inter-tribal war.

In 1881, the 'Childers' reforms (after Hugh Childers, Secretary of State for War) rationalised the regimental system, bringing Regulars, Militia and Volunteers together in one structure. Single battalion regiments were ordered to amalgamate in order to form two battalions of a 'new regiment'. For the 63rd this meant amalgamation with the 96th Regiment of Foot to form the 1st and 2nd Battalions Manchester Regiment. From this point onwards, the system of maintaining one battalion overseas and at a higher state of readiness for operations than the home-based battalion, worked well. The regimental depot at Ashton-under-Lyne was to provide a permanent home for the regiment and a strong link with the home population. The Militia Battalions became the 3rd (Reserve) and 4th (Extra Reserve) Battalions and, in due course, battalions of the Lancashire Rifle Volunteer Corps became 'Volunteer Battalions' of the regiment.

By the end of 1881, the new 1st Battalion Manchester Regiment had returned to the plains of India. They returned home in 1882 but en-route stayed in Egypt, guarding Ismailia during the brief campaign which ended in the Battle of Tel-El-Kebir. They remained in the United Kingdom for the next fifteen years. The 1st Battalion left its base at Gibraltar in August 1999, landing in South Africa in the middle of the following month. From Durban the battalion went direct to the small railway town of Ladysmith in Natal, then threatened by the invading Boers. Here they formed part of the heroic garrison of the town, which, during many long months, defied the Boer army. Later it took part in the big 'drives' which, carried out in combination with the blockhouse lines that had been widely established, gradually wore down the Boers and brought resistance to an end in early 1902.

The first regiment to bear the number 96 was raised in January 1761 and was sent immediately to India, where it served at Bombay and Madras, taking part in the reduction of Madura. With the end of the Seven Years' War in 1763, the army was reduced in strength and several regiments were disbanded. Amongst these was the 96th. When in 1803 the 32nd Regiment became Light Infantry, its second battalion was taken from it and numbered the 96th Regiment of Foot. Before the year was out, a second battalion had been raised to the new 96th. The 1st Battalion 96th Regiment served for a year in Ireland and was then sent to the West Indies, returning to England in 1816 and disbanding in December 1818. The 2nd Battalion of the 96th served in England and Jersey, disbanding in 1815.

In 1798, Britain occupied Minorca and found over 1,000 prisoners of war reputedly captured by the French from the Austrians in Italy, whom the French had literally sold to the Spanish at $2 a head. Although described as a Swiss regiment, it consisted of men of many different nationalities. The battalion was re-formed as the Minorca Regiment in 1800 and in 1801 was designated the Queen's German Regiment. The regiment fought with distinction at the Battle of Alexandria and throughout the Egyptian campaign against the French. In 1802 they returned to England, and in 1803 were in Ireland. In 1804 they were given the number 97th Regiment but retained the title of Queen's German Regiment. After action in the Peninsula under Wellington, the 97th returned to England and in February 1816, the 95th Rifles being taken out of the Line, the 97th was renumbered 96th. It was disbanded in December 1818.

A new 96th, which was to become the direct predecessor of the 2nd Manchesters, was raised five years later on 6 February 1824 at Salford Barracks, Manchester. It was allowed to carry the battle honours awarded to the previous 96th Regiment – Peninsula, Egypt and the Sphinx. The battalion moved to Canada in 1824, then to the West Indies the following year, where it remained for three years until returning to Canada. The 96th returned to England in 1835. Between then and 1839 it led a roving life between stations in England and Ireland. Between July 1840 and August 1841, the regiment sailed from England to New South Wales in twenty detachments guarding convict ships. Part of the regiment served in New Zealand, taking part in the war of 1845-47. In 1849 the 96th moved to India, remaining there until retuning to England and barracks in Ireland in 1855. In 1863 the regiment embarked for the Cape of Good Hope, remaining in South Africa for two years before moving to India, remaining there until 1874. The next few years were spent moving between a large number of locations in the United Kingdom.

In 1881, the amalgamation with the 63rd Regiment and the change of title to 2nd Battalion the Manchester Regiment took effect. The new 2nd Manchesters went to Malta that year and the final ten years of the nineteenth century kept the battalion fully occupied in its overseas role. They took part in the second Miranzai expedition on the north-west frontier of India during 1891, spent the next five years in India, followed by a year in Aden, then home to England – stationed in Manchester and in Lichfield. After exactly one year the battalion moved to Dublin, but the war in South Africa disrupted troop movements and the battalion was ordered to prepare for early embarkation to Egypt.

This instruction was cancelled on the day it was received and the 2nd Battalion moved to Aldershot, where they mobilised ready for active service in South Africa. They left Aldershot on 16 March and the battalion boarded the Bavarian at Southampton. Capetown was reached on 6 April and Port Elizabeth on the 10th. During the course of the war the battalion was constantly employed in mobile columns, in guarding the many blockhouses in the course of erection, and finally in the 'drives' which gradually wore down the opposition of the Boers. They returned to England and Aldershot in October 1902 before moving to the Channel Isles in June 1904.

In addition to the work carried out by the 1st and 2nd Battalions, to which the Volunteer Service Companies were attached, four other battalions of the Manchester Regiment were also involved in the war. In March 1900, six regiments of infantry were increased by two line battalions to be numbered 3rd and 4th Battalions respectively. The Manchester Regiment was one of those selected and, as a consequence, the existing 3rd and 4th Militia Battalions were renumbered as the 5th and 6th Battalions. These additional 3rd and 4th Battalions were disbanded in 1908 and the two Militia Battalions reverted to their original numbers.

In the Great War, the regiment expanded to forty-two battalions. Twenty-seven proceeded overseas and fought in all theatres of war – in France and Belgium, Italy and Salonika, Gallipoli and Egypt, Palestine and Mesopotamia – gaining seventy Battle Honours. Eleven Victoria Crosses were awarded to men of the regiment.

The years between the wars were not particularly peaceful, both the 1st and 2nd Battalions being involved in internal security operations in Iraq, Ireland, Palestine and Burma. The 2nd Battalion served in Mesopotamia (Iraq) in 1920, where Captain George Henderson was awarded a posthumous Victoria Cross. After service in India, the 2nd Battalion carried out intensive operations in aid of the civil power in Burma. The 1st Battalion spent several years in Ireland and later in Palestine on internal security duties before moving to Singapore in 1938.

The Territorial Battalions underwent many changes up to and including the Second World War. In 1922 the 6th and 7th Battalions amalgamated to form the 6th/7th Battalion, which became 65 Anti-Aircraft Regiment RA in December 1936. The 10th Battalion became 41st Battalion Royal Tank Corps in October 1938, renamed 41st Royal Tank Regiment in 1939. A 'second line' was formed at Oldham in April 1939 and numbered 47th Battalion RTR. Both battalions were in action in the Middle East. After the victory at El Alamein, the 47th, which had suffered appalling casualties, was disbanded. The 41st were then equipped with flail tanks and became 1st Scorpion Regiment RAC. Later they became 1st Assault (Engineer) Regiment.

In March 1939, the Territorial Army was doubled in strength and the 5th Battalion was divided in two, the second half forming a new 6th Battalion. A duplicate was raised at the same time by the 8th (Ardwick) Battalion to become the 7th Battalion. After serving with the BEF, the 5th Battalion was re-designated 111 Regiment Royal Armoured Corps (The Manchester Regiment) in November 1941. In November 1943 it reverted to infantry, converting to a machine-gun role. In August/September 1944, the regiment acted as the Royal Bodyguard at Balmoral. They were stationed in Malta from November 1945 until November 1946 before being disbanded in February 1947 and reformed as a Heavy Anti-Aircraft Regiment RA in 1947.

After the 1st Battalion had been taken prisoner at Singapore, a new 1st Battalion was formed in June 1942 by renumbering the new 6th Territorial Army Battalion as the 1st. The new 7th Battalion went to Belgium after D-Day in October 1944. After the war they returned to the UK and disbandment. The 8th (Ardwicks) and the 9th Battalion both mobilised in 1939 and went to France with the BEF. The 8th then went to Malta, serving there throughout the siege, then to the Middle East and Italy, where they fought until the end of the war with 10th Indian Division. The 9th went to Iceland as the medium machine-gun Battalion of 'C' Force in March 1941, then to Scotland, the Orkney and Shetland Islands, and later, in December 1942, to East Anglia. From there they went to Italy in 1943 as the machine-gun battalion of 4th Indian Division and later the 46th Division, and, eventually, to Klagenfurt, Austria. A 2nd/9th Battalion was raised in 1939 and became 88th Anti-Tank Regiment Royal Artillery in December 1941.

The new 1st Battalion saw active service in Europe after D-Day, ending the war in Hamburg, and the 2nd Battalion fought throughout the Burma campaign. After the war, the two regular battalions amalgamated to form a 1st Battalion (63/96). This battalion served in Germany between 1948 and 1951; in Malaya between 1951 and 1954; and again in Germany from 1954 until amalgamation with the King's Regiment in 1958. In 2005, this regiment was absorbed into a new Duke of Lancaster's Regiment.

The photographs forming the contents of this book are from the extensive Manchester Regiment photographic archive held in the Local Studies Library of Tameside Metropolitan Borough Council in Ashton-under-Lyne and my own personal collection, plus the photographs on pages 110 and 112 taken by Ian Hanson. The majority are published for the first time and I hope that this coverage from the very earliest days of the regiment will be of interest to the many thousands throughout the world who continue to take an interest in the history of this fine regiment.

Robert Bonner, 2011
The Museum of the Manchester Regiment

1

PRE-1881

1st Battalion colour belt worn by the ensign carrying the colour.

An unknown Grenadier Company Officer of the 63rd Regiment in 1775. His coat is scarlet with the lapels, cuffs and lining in the deep green facing colour of the 63rd Regiment. The Grenadier Company was picked from the tallest and strongest men of the regiment, and when on parade took station on the right of the line. In action, the Grenadiers were expected to lead assaults.

The 63rd Regiment first saw action in America at the Battle of Bunker Hill on 17 June 1775, where, by continuing to attack the enemy positions frontally, despite being twice driven back, the British established themselves on the heights, commanding Boston. The Grenadier and Light Companies of the 63rd were actively engaged in this action.

From the painting by James de Loutherbourg in the National Gallery of Scotland depicting Pte Antoine Lutz presenting Sir Ralph Abercrombie with the French standard, which he had captured at the Battle of Alexandria in 1801. Following its disbandment in 1818, the battle honours which this regiment had gained were bequeathed to the new 96th Regiment of 1823, eventually to become 2nd Battalion the Manchester Regiment.

The foundation of Perth, Western Australia, 12 August 1829. HMS *Sulphur* and the hired transport *Parmeila* sailed from England for the Swan River Settlement, arriving on 2 and 8 June 1829 respectively. A painting in the Western Art Gallery, Perth, Australia, shows the Governor reading the Declaration. On his right is Captain Frederick Chidley Irwin of the 63rd Regiment. An officer and soldiers of the 63rd Regiment are shown in the background. Captain Irwin later became the Lieutenant Governor and military commander of Western Australia.

A soldier of the 96th Regiment sent this portrait of himself on a letter to his sister 'In full uniform for Chatham Fair' just before his departure for Australia in 1840. The 96th Regiment had moved to Chatham in July 1839. Between 4 July 1840 and 15 August 1841, the regiment sailed in twenty separate detachments as guards on board convict ships to New South Wales and Tasmania.

The 63rd Regiment served in the Crimean War, making an unsuccessful forced march to reach the Alma in time for the battle. The regiment was present at the Battle of Balaklava and was hotly engaged at Inkerman on 5 November 1854, where it carried out a desperate charge. The Ensigns carrying the Colours were killed at the side of the Commanding Officer. The regiment was also present at the fall of Sevastopol.

In June 1855, at the end of the Crimean War, the 63rd Regiment sailed to Halifax, Nova Scotia. In April 1861, war broke out between the Northern and Southern States of America, and by November there was a possibility that Britain might become involved in hostilities with the Federal Government. In February 1862, the regiment was sent by sleighs to Rivière du Loup, then by train to Montreal and London, West Canada. They returned to Montreal in September 1864 and to England in August 1865.

During 1861, the 96th Regiment embarked on the steam transports *Victoria* and *Calcutta*, bound for Canada. The *Victoria* encountered bad weather and, within 120 miles of the Azores, the engines broke down and the ship took on water to a depth of 5-6ft in the engine room. The *Victoria*, with half of the regiment on board, returned to England. The *Calcutta* carried on to Canada but the four companies on board returned to England a few weeks later, rejoining the rest of the regiment at Shorncliffe, where it stayed between April 1862 and January 1863.

The 96th arrived at the Cape of Good Hope on 26 March 1863 and at first were stationed at Port Elizabeth, where this photograph of D Company in marching order was taken.

The band of the 96th in their white uniforms at Graham's Town in 1865. The Drum-Major is on the left with three band-boys sitting in the centre. Headquarters and three companies had arrived there in July 1864.

Lieutenant-Colonel the Hon. A.M. Cathcart and officers of the 96th at Graham's Town. Three, in scarlet tunics, are wearing the cap introduced in 1855, mounted with a 2in-diameter red and white woollen ball worn by officers of battalion companies. The other uniformed officers are wearing the 1855 pattern dark blue undress uniform with the undress forage cap. The 96th sailed to India in October/November 1865 with a strength of 1,078 all ranks.

In 1873, the 63rd and 96th Regiments were linked together, with their depot at Ashton-under-Lyne. To these two regular battalions were also affiliated the 6th Royal Lancashire Militia, the 4th and 7th Administrative Battalions Lancashire Rifle Volunteers, and the 6th, 33rd, 40th and 56th Lancashire Rifle Volunteers. The 63rd were in India at this time and the 96th had returned to England in 1873. Officers of the 96th are photographed here at Brentwood in 1875.

Left: Sergeant-Major Taylor of the 33rd Lancashire Rifle Volunteers, Ardwick, 1867. This unit had been formed in November 1859 as an 'Artizan Company of Riflemen'. In 1888 it was to be re-titled as the 5th Volunteer Battalion the Manchester Regiment and in 1908 as the 8th (Ardwick) Battalion the Manchester Regiment.

Below: Officers of the 96th Regiment at Aldershot in 1881, shortly before amalgamation with the 63rd Regiment. In 1874, officers had been given permission to wear the Sphinx with the word Egypt as the badge on their forage caps in recognition of the Battle Honour awarded to an earlier 96th Regiment.

2

1881-1900

In 1881 the 'Childers' reforms (after Hugh Childers, Secretary of State for War) rationalised the regimental and home command systems, bringing Regulars, Militia and Volunteers together in one structure. Single battalion regiments were ordered to amalgamate in order to form two battalions of a 'new regiment'. For the 63rd this meant amalgamation with the 96th Regiment of Foot to form the 1st and 2nd Battalions Manchester Regiment. From this point onwards, the system of maintaining one battalion overseas and at a higher state of readiness for operations than the home-based battalion worked well. The regimental depot at Ashton-under-Lyne was to provide a permanent home for the regiment and a strong link with the home population. The Militia became the 3rd (Reserve) and 4th (Extra Reserve) Battalions. Between 1888 and 1890, battalions of the Lancashire Rifle Volunteer Corps became the 1st to 6th Volunteer Battalions of the regiment and in 1908 were re-designated as battalions of the Territorial Force.

Left: Sergeant Master-Tailor Lister, Sergeant-Major Eales and Band-Sergeant Waterfield. They were the last three NCOs of the old 63rd Regiment still serving with the 1st Battalion in 1893.

Below: Following months of unrest in Egypt, an expeditionary force was sent out from England and Malta to Alexandria in August 1882. During the two months that the campaign lasted, the 2nd Battalion remained in Alexandria; one of their duties being to guard the Arsenal. They were later joined by their wives and children, and men under twenty years of age, all having been left behind in Malta. The battalion embarked for India on 14/15 October 1882 aboard *Euphrates* and *Adjutant*, with 776 officers, rank and file, women and children.

Men of the 2nd Battalion waiting in the rain at the Grand Durbar Camp, held at Rawalpindi in March 1885. Some 18,500 troops had assembled to parade before the Amir of Afghanistan and the Viceroy of India.

The 4th Regiment of Royal Lancashire Militia became, in 1881, the 3rd and 4th Battalions of the Manchester Regiment and were the first battalions of the Manchester Regiment to serve at Ashton-under-Lyne when the Regimental Depot was established there that same year. The Officers, Warrant-Officers and Sergeants of the two Militia Battalions are shown in a group at the Regimental Depot in 1887.

Lieutenant-Colonel Henry L. Rocca was born in Hamburg, Germany, on 29 April 1831. He came to England in 1851, settling in Manchester, and became a naturalised British subject (later becoming principal of a firm of merchants and shippers). He joined the 33rd Lancashire Rifle Volunteer Corps (2nd Manchester) in 1866 and, although offered a commission, insisted in drilling in the ranks until proficient. He was gazetted Lieutenant on 19 November 1869 and eventually made Lieutenant-Colonel, commanding the Ardwick Battalion on 10 January 1885. His son, Frederic, was killed in action as a Sergeant with the 20th Manchesters in 1916.

Lieutenant-Colonel Rocca, his officers of the Ardwick Battalion and families relaxing at camp in 1891. The evolution of the annual camp provided Volunteers with the opportunity of realistic training in military affairs and the benefit of fresh air and exercise away from the city. Although primarily of a military nature, they also took part in major social events. Such was the popularity of these camps that wives and families would visit for the day, usually on the middle Sunday of the month. It was a real 'day out' to see the Volunteers.

The 2nd Battalion had been stationed in India since November 1883; in 1891 there were two punitive expeditions to the Miranzai Valley in the North-West Frontier. Three companies of the battalion took part in the second campaign, which consisted mainly of marching through villages, showing the flag, and persuading the tribesmen to submit. This peaceful camp scene belies the tough conditions and the hostile environment in which the soldiers took part.

The 2nd Manchesters marched out from Meerut to Chakrata, North-West Province, in March 1893 and remained there throughout the hot weather. In August they rehearsed a *feu de joie* in preparation for the birthday of Queen Victoria, the Queen Empress.

Officers' Mess, Chakrata, 1893.

Soldiers of the 1st Battalion exercising with rifles, Limerick, 1893. The band and drums played when this was carried out by the whole battalion, creating a rhythmic and spectacular display. The battalion had been stationed in Ireland since 1888, with headquarters at Tipperary, then Kinsale; it remained in Ireland until October 1894.

In November 1893, the 2nd Battalion went by march, river and rail to Dinapore. During their stay in the garrison, the battalion lost one sergeant and fourteen men in an outbreak of cholera which occurred in August 1894. A further two officers, seven Non-Commissioned Officers, thirty-two men and seven children all died during their stay in Dinapore.

Pigsticking party, Agra, India, 1894. Standing, from left to right: Captains C.C. Melvill, G.W. Fitton, R.D. Vizard, J.E. Watson and E.A. Ward. Seated: A.H. Baldwin, C.P. Ridley and L.H. Prioleau.

The Subaltern Officers of the 2nd Battalion at Dinapore in 1894. Standing, from left to right: D.A.D. McVean, H.O. Lash, D.R. Paton, A.E. Sealy, A.N. Hood, E.G. Broomhead, A. Menzies, W. Bolland, H.M.W. Souter, G.C. Cooper-King, J. Stevens and C.G. Stansfield. Seated: R.S. Weston, E. Vaughan, E.H. Gorges and A.W.V. Plunkett. A.W.V. Plunkett, later as Lieutenant-Colonel, commanded 2nd King's African Rifles. He was killed in action at Gumburu, Somalia on 17 April 1903. A bronze memorial to his memory is located in Manchester Cathedral.

The 2nd Battalion on Guard at Fort Gnatong, Sikkim, 1894. This was the highest post in the world occupied by British troops and the Quarter Guard wore balaclava caps, snow-goggles, thick-lined greatcoats, warm gloves, blue serge trousers, khaki puttees and boots. Thirty years later, in 1924, the 2nd Battalion occupied this post once again, prior to its being taken over by the Indian Police.

Above: A lunch party at Agra in 1894.

Right: The Captains of the 2nd Battalion relaxing at Dinapore in 1894. From left to right: A.B. Maxwell, J.E. Watson, J.H. Abbot-Anderson, R.D. Vizard, -?-. All went on to become Lieutenant-Colonels and Abbot-Anderson, as Colonel, became the Commandant of the Peking Legation Garrison Guard between 1906 and 1911.

The 1st Battalion spent two years at Aldershot, between November 1895 and November 1897, occupying Barrosa Barracks, Stanhope Lines, South Camp. Captain C.S. Cottingham was the Transport Officer and responsible for stable routine, the proper care of horses and mules, the fit and general condition of the harness and the general turnout of the Transport on parade.

Barrosa Barracks, Aldershot. Standing, from left to right: the Band Sergeant, Farrier Sergeant (wearing pill box hat), Armourer Sergeant, Orderly-Room Sergeant, Pioneer Sergeant and the Drum-Major. Seated: the Regimental Quartermaster-Sergeant, the Regimental Sergeant-Major, the Quartermaster, the Sergeant Instructor of Musketry and the Bandmaster.

Barrosa Barracks, Aldershot. The Adjutant with the Drum-Major and the Corp of Drums. Three Drummer Boys are sitting at the front. During the Boer War, the big drum in the photograph had been stored at Ladysmith in the tent of the Sergeant-Major, where it was hit by splinters from a shell fired by the Boer 'Long Tom' gun. The drum survived and is now in the Manchester Regiment Museum.

Barrosa Barracks, Aldershot. Sergeant Master-Tailor Tigh with his staff, including two boy tailors.

Left: Apart from drill, marksmanship was the most important activity of the Volunteers. Major Heap of the 2nd Volunteer Battalion, winner at Bisley in 1897 of the Alexandra Cup, the Grand Aggregate Bronze Cross and the English Twenty, is seen here wearing his Marksman and Best Shot badges.

Below: Officers of the 2nd Battalion in different forms of dress at Thubba, 1890.

3

THE ANGLO-BOER WAR

The following battalions of the regiment took part in the Anglo-Boer War:

1st Battalion   2nd Battalion
3rd Battalion   4th Battalion
5th (Militia) Battalion   6th (Militia) Battalion

Four Volunteer Service Companies went to the war, provided by men from the following:

1st Volunteer Battalion (Wigan), 2nd Volunteer Battalion (Stretford Road),
3rd Volunteer Battalion (Ashton-under-Lyne), 4th Volunteer Battalion (Burlington Street),
5th Volunteer Battalion (Ardwick) and 6th Volunteer Battalion (Oldham).

The 1st Manchesters were part of the Gibraltar Garrison when war broke out in South Africa. On arrival they were sent to Ladysmith, which came under siege from the Boers in November 1899. Caesar's Camp, which constituted C Sector of the Ladysmith defences, was recognised as the key to Ladysmith, and the Manchesters were proud of the distinction of holding it. The Manchesters' tented camp at Caesar's Camp lay sheltered on the reverse of the height, with the front line just a few yards beyond, over the skyline.

Despite constant battles during the siege of Ladysmith opportunities were taken for the occasional game of cricket between the defending units. The battalion cricket team proudly wore the fleur-de-lys on their shirts.

Large numbers of reservists were called-up in February 1900 and were sent to the Hulme Cavalry Barracks, Manchester. Shown are some of the 2nd Battalion Officers who were responsible for their training.

Officers of various Manchester Regiment battalions assembled at Aldershot in March 1900, prior to embarkation to join their respective battalions in South Africa. From left to right, back row: 2nd-Lt H.O. Carroll (3rd), Lt King-Pearce (2nd), 2nd-Lt D. Morley (4th), 2nd-Lt E.L. Makin (4th), 2nd-Lt C.M. Thornycroft (2nd), 2nd-Lt W.C.N. Hastings (2nd), 2nd-Lt H.C. Bates (4th). Standing: Surgeon Captain Black (RAMC), Capt. G.C. Cooper-King (2nd), Lt F.S. Nisbet (2nd), Lt F.H. Dorling (2nd), Capt. D.C. Ansted (5th Militia), Lt C.F.H. Trueman (2nd), Captain (QM) Stewart-Wynne (2nd), Capt. W.H. Goldfinch (2nd), Lt J.D.B. Erskine (2nd). Sitting: Captain and Adj. J.H.M. Jebb (2nd), Capt. W.H. Williamson (2nd), Maj. L.H. Prioleau (3rd), Lt-Col. C.J. Reay (2nd), Lt-Col. J.P. Gethin (3rd), Maj. J.H. Abbott-Anderson (2nd), Capt. H.L. James (2nd). Sitting on the ground: 2nd-Lt H. Knox (3rd), 2nd-Lt W.G.K.P. Bayley (4th), 2nd-Lt Napier (6th Militia), 2nd-Lt P.D. de la Penrha (2nd), Nai Trum (Siamese Army).

Inspection of the 2nd Battalion on the dockside after disembarking in South Africa, April 1900.

Manchesters of the 1st Volunteer Service Company manning a blockhouse at Natalspruit. From left to right are Sgt Alfred Walmsley, L/Cpl A.W. Donnelly, Pte Chadderton and L/Cpl W. Coe.

Clegg Street Station, Oldham, on Saturday, 5 May 1900. Lieutenant Percy Bamford and his section from the 6th Volunteer Battalion prepare for the first leg of their journey to South Africa. From left to right: Lt P. Bamford, Sgt J.H. Barr, Pte G.H. Bowden, Pte W. Dolphyn, Pte William Emmott, Pte T. Kershaw, Pte H. Ogden, Pte A. Taylor, Pte P. Taylor, Pte T. Wadsworth and Pte R. Weston.

Lieutenant Hardwick and men of the 4th Volunteer Battalion of Burlington Street, Manchester, who were the first to volunteer their services for the Imperial Yeomanry in January 1900.

In South Africa, infantry battalions had to detach complete companies to act as Mounted Infantry in order to compete with the mobility of the Boers, who owned their own horses and fought as fast-moving mounted units. Mounted Infantry were essentially infantry who rode into battle and then dismounted to fight the enemy. They were not intended to replace the regular cavalry and had an entirely different role to carry out. Mounted infantrymen travelled light and neither tents nor comforts were permitted for officers or men. Each man carried on his horse 120 rounds of ammunition, a spare shirt, a pair of socks, underpants, a holdall, boot laces, sponge, towel, soap, a rubber curry comb and brush, a water bottle, an emergency ration and one day's supply of oats for his horse.

A Galloper gun of the 2nd Battalion Mounted Infantry Company ready for action.

For the soldiers of all the battalions, much of their time was spent 'on trek': mile after mile on the veldt, with the occasional ride on the company or battalion horse- or mule-drawn transport.

Men of the 1st Volunteer Service Company at Schoeman's Kloof. From left to right: Pte Albert Priest, Pte W. Cunliffe, Pte G. Roberts, Pte Henry Hindley, Pte H. Ogden, -?-, L/Cpl Walworth, Pte W. Dolphyn. Seated centre: Pte Patrick Connolly and Pte A. Bate.

The 1st Battalion Mounted Infantry Company at rest. A green cloth regimental fleur-de-lys can be seen on the left side of some helmets.

A Company of the 2nd Manchesters in South Africa.

Above: Second Lieutenant Ellershaw of 1st Manchesters showing his rifle to General E.S. Brook and explaining that it could not be repaired by the armourer. Lieutenants C.F. Boone, G.S. Routley and J.F. Oliver are on the left, with Capt. Thomson, ADC to the General, on the right.

Right: Approximately 8,000 blockhouses and other fortifications were erected across the length and breadth of South Africa. This particularly strong blockhouse of two storeys near Bethlehem was used by the Manchesters as a command post.

A certificate presented by the local authority in Wigan to members of the 1st Volunteer Battalion who had served in South Africa.

A certificate presented by Colonel Higson and the officers of the 1st Volunteer Battalion to those members of the unit who had served in South Africa. Most of the Volunteers who had served in the war were presented by their battalions or local authority with commemorative items such as battalion medals and silver tobacco boxes.

London Road Station (now Piccadilly) where the waiting crowds assembled to welcome the returning members of one of the Volunteer Service Companies.

Crowds came out in strength to welcome home the 1st Volunteer Service Company as they marched through Piccadilly Gardens led by Capt. B.C.P. Heywood and Lieutenants H.C. Darlington and P. Bamford on 24 May 1901.

Manchester's principal South African war memorial was unveiled in St Ann's Square in October 1908, almost six years since the start of discussions to raise a memorial. General Sir Ian Hamilton recalled the heroic deeds of the Manchester Regiment in South Africa, including their battle at Elandslaagte, before he removed the Union Flag covering the memorial. A Guard of Honour was provided by the 2nd Battalion.

4

1892-1914

Battle Honours prior to 1914:

The Sphinx superscribed 'Egypt'.
Guadeloupe 1759, Egmont op Zee, Peninsula, Martinique 1809, Guadeloupe 1810, New Zealand, Alma, Inkerman, Sevastopol, Afghanistan 1879-80, Egypt 1882, Defence of Ladysmith, South Africa 1899-1902.

The 2nd Volunteer Battalion on the sands at Blackpool, 1897.

The band of the 2nd Battalion, Bulford Camp, Aldershot, August 1899.

Right: The 2nd Volunteer Battalion Mounted Infantry Company in camp at Lytham in 1903.

Below: The 3rd Battalion went to St Helena in July 1902 to guard Boer prisoners of war. In December, the battalion – less two companies remaining in St Helena – embarked for Capetown and from there went to Middleburg, Transvaal, where they remained until September 1906. Here two machine-gun sections of the battalion display their weapons.

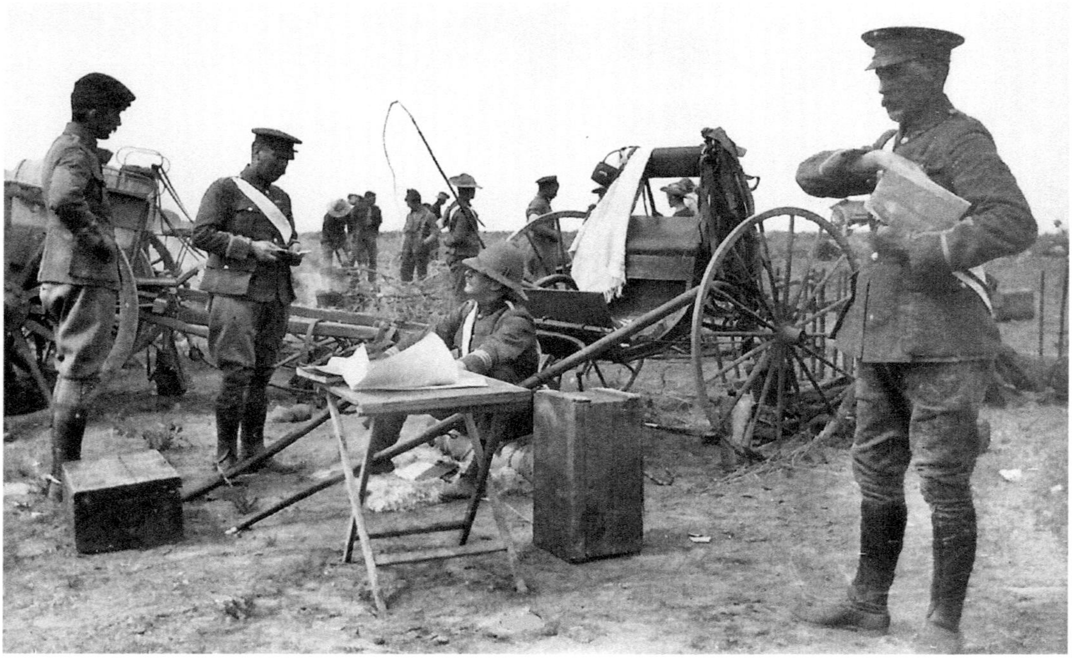

A consultation on manoeuvres between officers of the 3rd Battalion: Adjutant, Commanding Officer, Quartermaster (seated) and the Transport Officer, Donkerspoort, South Africa, 18 September 1905.

Men of the 3rd Battalion building a bridge over a river-bed on the veldt.

Five Warrant Officers from 1st Battalion, Secunderabad, India in 1905. Standing, from left to right: C. Joyce, J.J. Haddon DCM, G. Prosser DCM. Sitting: Patrick O'Brien (later Major QM and father of Major (QM) Herbert O'Brien MBE), and William Lawrence Connery (son of Colonel (QM) Michael H. Connery MC) and later Lt-Col. (QM), Mayor of Ashton-under-Lyne and father of L.T.M. Connery and F.A.J. Connery, both commissioned in the 9th Battalion.

The Mounted Infantry Platoon of the 1st Battalion at Secunderabad, India in 1905, wearing the unpopular Brodrick cap named after the then Secretary of State for War. It was similar in shape to that worn by sailors, of blue cloth with a semi-circular patch of white facings in front on which the regimental badge was worn.

A photograph of all those still serving in 1906 in the 2nd Battalion in Secunderabad who had served in the Boer War. All are wearing their Queen's South Africa or King's South Africa medals or both. From left to right, back row: L/Cpl Hollock, Cpl Maloney, Pte Newall, Pte Mathews, Pte King, Pte Farrow, Pte Shaw, Pte Upton, Pte McKenna, Pte Fitton. Middle row: Sgt Grant, Sgt Watson, Sgt Holland, Sgt Johnson, Sgt Tallentine, Col.-Sgt T. Milner, L/Cpl Ledward, Sgt Kennedy, Pte Milne, Sgt Yeates, Sgt Chase. Front row: Col.-Sgt J.T. Milner, Col.-Sgt Eldon, Frazeer, QMS Pike, Col. R.D. Vizard, QMS Finney, Col.-Sgt Danvers, Col.-Sgt Kean, Col.-Sgt Wilson.

The 2nd Battalion cricket team of 1906 at Guernsey. Standing: -?-, Thorning, Capt. C.F.H. Trueman, -?-, Lt C.A. Bolton, Capt. E.R. Cockburn. Seated: Capt. F.S. Nisbet, Lt-Col. J.E. Watson, 2nd-Lt H.T.R.S. Wright. On the ground: 2nd-Lt J.S. Harper, Lt C.D. Irwin, 2nd-Lt C.H. Gibson, Lt C.W. Wood.

Left: Colour-Sergeant George H. Guest of the 2nd Volunteer Battalion Mounted Infantry Company in 1907. He served with the Company for twenty years from its start in 1888 through to its disbandment in 1908.

Below: Captain O. St Leger Davies of the 2nd Volunteer Battalion Mounted Infantry Company (centre) with Lt H.T. Cawley, Lt J.W. Barclay and his Non-Commissioned Officers at Windmill Hill annual camp in 1906.

The 4th Battalion had been raised at Aldershot in March 1900 and was used as a draft-producing unit during the Boer War. It moved to Kinsale in Ireland in 1901 and remained there until returning to Aldershot in October 1905. Here the battalion is returning to camp after manoeuvres near Aldershot. The battalion was disbanded in December 1906.

A Company 1st Battalion, Kamptee, India in 1910, commanded by Capt. W.C.N. Hastings DSO. Private Issy Smith, later to be awarded the VC in the First World War, is circled. As Lieutenant-Colonel in the First World War, Hastings commanded the Sierra Leone Battalion West African Frontier Force and took part in the Cameroon Campaign of 1915/16.

Above: Lieutenant Brodie Valentine Mair and the 1st Battalion Signallers at Kamptee in 1910. As Captain with the 1st Battalion in the First World War he was awarded the Distinguished Service Order and the Military Cross and bar. He died in Waziristan, India in May 1922.

Right: Lieutenant-Colonel Robert Davenport Vizard commanded the 1st Manchesters in India between 1908 and 1910.

The Review Day of the Delhi Durbar, attended by King George V, 14 December 1911. The march-past of the Jullundur Brigade in review order, Manchester Regiment, 28th Punjabis, 47th Sikhs and 53rd Sikhs (Frontier Force): 50,000 men in total.

5

THE GREAT WAR, 1914-1918

First World War Battle Honours:

1st Battalion
La Bassee 1914, Armentières 1914, Givenchy 1914, Neuve Chapelle, Ypres 1915, St Julien, Aubers, Bazentin, Megiddo, Sharon, Tigris 1916, Kut, Baghdad.

2nd Battalion
Mons, Le Cateau, Retreat from Mons, Marne 1914, Aisne 1914 La Bassee 1914, Armentières, Ypres 1915, Gravenstafel, Frezenberg, Bellewaarde, Somme 1916, Albert 1916, Sambre, Ancre 1918, Amiens, Hindenburg Line, St Quentin Canal.

5th Battalion
Helles, Krithia, Rumani, Albert, Ypres 1917, Somme 1918, Bapaume, Arras, Ancre, Hindenburg Line, Canal du Nord, Cambrai 1918, Selle, Sambre.

2nd /5th Battalion
Ypres 1917, Poelcapelle, St Quentin, Somme 1918.

6th Battalion
Helles, Krithia, Rumani, Ypres 1917, Arras 1918, Somme 1918, Albert 1918, Bapaume1918, Hindenburg Line, Canal du Nord, Cambrai, Selle.

2nd /6th Battalion
Ypres 1917, Poelcapelle, St Quentin, Rosières.

7th Battalion
Helles, Krithia, Rumani, Ypres 1917, Arras 1918, Somme 1918, Albert 1918, Bapame 1918, Hindenburg Line, Canal du Nord.

2nd /7th Battalion
Ypres 1917, Poelcapelle, St Quentin, Rosières.

8th Battalion
Helles, Krithia, Rumani, Ypres 1918, Somme 1918, Arras 1918, Ancre 1918, Albert 1918, Bapaume 1918, Hindenburg Line, Canal du Nord, Cambrai 1918, Selle, Sambre.

2nd /8th Battalion
Ypres 1917, Poelcapelle.

9th Battalion
Krithia, Rumani, Ypres 1917.

2nd /9th Battalion
Ypres 1917, Poelcapelle, Somme 1918,
Rosières, Hindenburg Line, Cambrai.

10th Battalion
Helles, Krithia, Rumani, Somme 1918,
Bapaume, Albert 1918, Canal du Nord,
Selle.

2nd /10th Battalion
Ypres 1917, Poelcapelle.

11th Battalion
Suvla, Landing at Suvla, Scimitar Hill,
Somme 1916, Flers Courcelette, Thiepval
Ancre Heights, Messines 1917, Ypres
1917, Langemarck 1917, Broodseinde
Hindenburg Line, Cambrai.

12th Battalion
Somme 1916, Albert, Delville Wood,
Arras 1917, Ypres 1917, Passchendaele,
Somme 1918, St Quentin, Bapaume,
Amiens, Albert 1918, Hindenburg Line,
Epechy, Selle, Sambre.

13th Battalion
Doiran 1917.

16th Battalion
Somme 1916, Albert, Transloy, Arras
1917, Ypres 1917, Pilckem, Somme 1918,
St Quentin, Lys, Kemmel, Ypres 1918,
Courtrai.

17th Battalion
Somme 1916, Albert, Transloy, Arras
1917, Scarpe 1917, Ypres 1917,Pilckem,
Somme 1918, St Quentin, Lys, Kemmel.

18th Battalion
Somme 1916, Albert, Transloy, Arras
1917, Scarpe 1917, Ypres 1917, Pilckem,
Passchendaele.

19th Battalion
Somme 1916, Albert, Arras 1917, Scarpe
1917, Ypres 1917.

20th Battalion
Somme 1916, Albert, Bazentin, Guillemont,
Bullecourt, Ypres 1917, Polygon Wood,
Broodseinde, Passchendaele, Beaurevoir,
Selle.

21st Battalion
Somme 1916, Albert, Bazentin,
Delville Wood, Bullecourt, Ypres 1917,
Broodseinde Passchendaele, Beaurevoir,
Cambrai 1918, Selle, Sambre, Piave.

22nd Battalion
Somme 1916, Albert, Bazentin, Delville
Wood, Guillemont, Bullecourt, Ypres 1917
Polygon Wood, Broodseinde, Piave, Vittorio
Veneto.

23rd Battalion
Somme 1916, Ypres 1917.

24th Battalion
Somme 1916, Albert, Bazentin, Delville
Wood, Guillemont, Bullecourt, Ypres
1917, Polygon Wood, Menin Road, Piave,
Vittorio Veneto.

Volunteers for the 1st City 'Pals' Battalion march into Heaton Park, Manchester, on the afternoon of Saturday, 12 September 1914. This battalion was later re-titled the 16th Battalion the Manchester Regiment and particularly distinguished itself at the Battle of Manchester Hill, Francilly-Selency, in March 1918.

A group of the first volunteers for the Pals Battalion erecting their tents in Heaton Park, Manchester.

Above: In uniform for the first time. There had been a nationwide shortage of khaki material following the outbreak of war and in the early days men were issued with blue uniforms. This was a very unpopular but short-term solution. The Pals were inspected at Heaton Park by Sir Henry Mackinnon on 1 December 1914.

Left: Ready to go to war. 'Boy' Ben Adams and his father of the 8th (Ardwick) Battalion in 1914.

Above: Company Officers with the band and drums of the 8th Battalion in Cyprus and the Mayor of Limassol, 16 December 1914. Note the boy soldier.

Right: Lieutenant-Colonel H.E. Gresham, standing in the centre, with officers of the 7th Battalion in Khartoum, Sudan, December 1914. The Adjutant, Major W.P.E. Newbigging DSO, is on the right. The battalion remained in Khartoum until transferring to Egypt in April 1915.

The 2nd Battalion had been stationed in Ireland since September 1902. This company group was photographed at the Curragh shortly before leaving for France on 13 August 1914.

On 13 August 1914 the 2nd Battalion entrained for Dublin. It left Ireland the following day aboard Buteshire for Le Havre. Strength 27 officers, 1 warrant-officer, 50 sergeants and 927 other ranks

Right: Wilfred Owen, arguably the greatest poet to emerge from the Great War, was commissioned into the Manchester Regiment in 1917. He was awarded the Military Cross for his bravery with 2nd Manchesters but was killed by machine-gun fire while leading his men across the Sambre Canal on 4 November 1918. A week later the Armistice was signed. A plaque in his memory, erected by the Wilfred Owen Association, is positioned on the bridge over the canal at Ors. A plaque in the Regimental Chapel in Manchester Cathedral also commemorates the life and death of the soldier poet.

Below: Lieutenant-Colonel W.G. Heys (centre with service dress cap) and a company of the 8th (Ardwick) Battalion at Alexandria before going to Gallipoli. Heys had served as a Captain during the Boer War with the 2nd Volunteer Service Company attached to 2nd Manchesters.

Men of the 6th Battalion resting in the desert near Alexandria, December 1914.

Lt-Col. G.G.P. Heywood, seated centre holding service dress cap, with the 6th Battalion warrant-officers and sergeants at Alexandria on 26 December 1914. Seated fifth from left is Captain and Adjutant P.V. Holberton, later as lieutenant-colonel he was killed in action on 26 March 1918 commanding the 5th Lancashire Fusiliers. Many of these Territorial Army soldiers wear their medal ribbons for previous service as volunteers in the Boer War.

Men of the 6th Battalion cleaning up after a disturbed night in a reserve line trench at Gallipoli in June 1915.

Sheltering in a rear trench at Gallipoli but prepared for anything.

Having completed their training in May 1916, this draft for the 20th Battalion is ready to join their battalion in France. This battalion went on to Italy in November 1917, returning to France and the Western Front in September 1918. Their last action was on 6 November 1918 at Dompierre, finishing the war on 11 November 1918 in Landrecies.

Opposite above: 2nd Battalion Headquarters, The Bluff, Ypres, June 1915. Lieutenants A.B. Close-Brooks and A.J. Scully, Captain C.M. Thornycroft, Lieutenants E.R. Vanderspar, W.W. Smith (KSLI) and K.S. Torrance. Close-Brooks, Scully and Torrance were each later awarded the Military Cross. Vanderspar died of his wounds on 24 June 1915 and Close-Brooks died of his wounds on 10 January 1917. Thornycroft, later as lieutenant-colonel, commanded the 2/9th Manchesters in 1917, then the 3rd (Special Reserve) Battalion. He was awarded the DSO in 1916 and appointed CBE in 1919.

Opposite below: Soldiers of the 11th Battalion shortly after coming out of the front line trenches near Serre in January 1917.

Lieutenant-Colonel Wilfrith Elstob DSO MC, seated centre, and the officers of the 16th Battalion at Reninghelst, near Poperinghe, January 1918. On 21 March, Elstob commanded his battalion during the Battle of Manchester Hill, where he was killed and later awarded a posthumous Victoria Cross.

Men of the 20th Battalion resting beside a disabled tank after the battle.

6

BETWEEN THE WARS, 1919-1939

In 1923, permission was given for the restoration of the fleur-de-lys of the 63rd Regiment to be worn as a regimental badge. This was welcomed throughout the regiment, replacing the Arms of the City of Manchester, which had been taken into use in 1881 following the renaming of the combined 63rd and 96th Regiments.

The war is over. The Colours of the 2nd Battalion are brought from England to join the battalion at Froidchapelle, France.

Officers of the 1st and 2nd Battalions, Farnham, 13 October 1919. From left to right, back row: Capt. G.E. Allen, Capt. G.S. Henderson DSO MC, Capt. H.R.C. Green, Lt C.D. Bruce, Capt. M.R. Davidson, Lt J.A. Caldwell, Maj. A.J. Scully MC, Lt G.D. Moorhead MC, Lt W.T. Williams-Green MC, Lt E.F. Orgill MC, Lt S.E. Hollins, Lt C.H. Keitley OBE. Third row: Lt E.E.J. Henderson, Lt A.G. Chittenden, Lt B. Burkett-Gottwalz, Lt G.M. Johnstone, Lt J.S. Partington, 2nd-Lt G. Hawke, Maj. A.E. O'Meara, Maj. C.D. Irwin MC, Lt J.B. Barker MC, Capt. A.W.U. Moore, Capt. N.S. Ince MC, Lt W. Clifford, Capt. J. Thompson, Lt T.W. Wynne MM. Second row: Lt H.D.C. Pearse MC, Lt E. Greer, Lt W. Coleshill MC, Maj. J.R. Heelis MC, Capt. E.L. Musson DSO MC, Lt-Col. E. Vaughan CMG DSO, Lt-Col. B.A. Wright DSO, Capt. H.G. Harrison, Maj. C.C. Stapledon, Capt. G.B. Martin MC, Lt J.R. Nicholson, Lt (QM) D.A. Carter DCM. Front row: 2nd-Lt J.W. Smith, Lt E.V. Hollingworth, Capt. G.M. Glover MC, Lt H.A. Webster, Lt J. Kelsey MC, Lt F. Hammond, 2nd-Lt J.A. Mason, Lt M.D. Pleasance MM, 2nd-Lt G.L. Morgan, Lt H. Makinson, Lt C. Cassidy.

Captain G.S. Henderson DSO MC was later awarded a posthumous Victoria Cross for his bravery during the Battle of Hillah, which took place in Mesopotamia on 24 July 1920.

Opposite below: The cadre of the 8th Battalion embarked from France on the *Mogileff* for home and Ardwick at 1600 hours on 4 April 1919. The weather was bright and warm, with every prospect of a comfortable crossing. The final stage in their long adventure of the world war was completed when they arrived in Manchester and, led by the Quartermaster Captain W.H. Stewart, amidst a tremendous and enthusiastic concourse of Mancunians, proudly made their way to even larger crowds awaiting their return at Ardwick Green.

Following the Government of Ireland Act of 1920, Belfast gained an unexpected status as a provincial capital. The inauguration of the Parliament on 22 June 1921 by King George V and its first full session the following day took place in the City Hall. Men of the 2nd Manchesters are shown lining the route and presenting arms to the royal party.

Opposite below: The wedding reception party of Colour-Sergeant Smith of the 2nd Battalion and Army Schoolmistress Miss M.M. Waters at Jullunder in 1923. At the back: CQMS Burley, WO (I) Redburn, Lt (QM) Carter. Standing: RQMS F.M. Lewis, Maj. A.G.M. Hardingham, Lt-Col. W.B. Eddowes, CQMS Harvey, RSM F. Snow DCM, Mrs Hardingham, Capt. E.B. Holmes MC. Seated: Mrs Lewis, Mrs Burley, Colour-Sergeant Smith, Mrs Smith, Miss House, Mrs Holmes, Mrs Carter.

The 2nd Battalion marches into the Curragh Camp, Ireland, led by the Corp of Drums and the band, 1922.

Lieutenant-Colonel W.B. Eddowes with the Warrant Officers and Sergeants of the 2nd Battalion at Jubbulpore in 1924, on the occasion of the celebration of the centenary of the 2nd Battalion 1824–1924. From left to right, seated: CSMs Redwood, C.D. Coleman DCM, Thomason, Maj. J.R. Heelis MC, RSM F. Snow DCM, Lt-Col. W.B. Eddowes, Lt Whyte, Lt (QM) Carter DCM, RQMS Lewis, CSM Allen. Second row: CQMSs Brown, Gebbart, Burley, Horsley, Sergeants J. Currie, Blower, Hughes, Gardner, CSM Ward, CQMS Harvey, Col.-Sgt Smith. Third row: Sergeants Herbert O'Brien, Murphy, Smith, Hanley, Frazer, Walton, Green, Barlow, Bushby, Lyons. Fourth row: Sergeants Moyahan, Walker, Nixon, Webster, Casey, Johnson, Cartwright, Maloney, Hirst. Fifth row: Band Sergeant Crofts, Sergeants Lakin, Ashton, Eccles, QMS Duffield (AOC), Sergeants J. Currie, Gerrity, Elliot, J. Cook DCM, Askew.

The Regimental Officers' Dinner Club, London, 16 June 1926. General Sir Herbert Lawrence, Colonel of the Regiment, presided.

The 2nd Battalion Colour Party, Maymo, Burma, 8 October 1929. Pictured are CQMS Henderson, Lt J.M.T.F. Churchill, CQMS Frazer, 2nd-Lt T.B.L. Churchill and CQMS Maloney on the occasion of the farewell parade to the Commanding Officer Lt-Col. J.R. Heelis MC. Both Churchill brothers, Tom and Jack, became famous commando leaders in the Second World War.

The 2nd Battalion Guard of Honour for the visit of Lord Irwin, the Viceroy of India at Falaknuma Palace, Hyderabad, where he was staying with the Nizam of Hyderabad. Maj. C.S. Tuely commanded the Guard of Honour, 16 December 1929.

Above: Following his recent appointment as Colonel-in-Chief, King George V and Queen Mary welcomed Lt-Col. Freyberg and officers of the regiment to Buckingham Palace on 16 May 1930.

Left: Lieutenant-Colonel Bernard Freyberg VC CMG DSO, commanding the 1st Battalion, with King George V.

Above: Regimental Sergeant-Major Mutters MC DCM MM with the Warrant-Officers and Sergeants of the Regimental Depot, June 1931. From left to right, standing: Sergeants Brazier, J. Knight, Derwood, W.C. Thomas, Wood, Garlick, Bailey, Kelly, C. Elliott, Wrenshaw, Wright (schoolmaster). Seated: Mr Hammond, Mr Frazer, Sgt J. Stridgeon DCM, CSM Cooper, CSM Allen, RSM Mutters, RQMS Yates, CSM Marland, Col.-Sgt Potts, Mr Cooper, Mr Lewis.

Right: Regimental Sergeant-Major 'Charlie' Mutters. He was a remarkable fighting soldier who enlisted in the regiment in 1908. During the First World War he was awarded the Military Medal in 1916; a bar to it in 1917; and the Distinguished Conduct Medal and the Military Cross in 1918. The Belgian Government honoured him with the Croix de Guerre in 1918. In July 1920 he was a Company Sergeant-Major with the 2nd Battalion at the Battle of Hillah in Mesopotamia. He retired in 1931. During the Second World War he became a Captain in the Home Guard.

B Company of the 2nd Battalion march-past, Trimulgherry, Secunderabad. The King's Colour is carried by Lt T.B.L. Churchill and the Regimental Colour by 2nd-Lt C.H.R. Hyde. In front are Lieutenants F. Egan and E.B. Holmes, Maj. Charles Tuely and 2nd-Lt J.M.T. Churchill. Behind the three companies of Manchesters are the 4/14th Punjab Regiment, 3/16th Punjab Regiment and the 3/6th Rajputana Rifles.

Sergeant J. Brammall and 11 Platoon, C Company on outpost duty at Nga Kuaing, Burma in 1932. The 2nd Battalion had been sent from India to Burma in May 1931 to work with the Burma Police in quelling an open rebellion against the government by a large number of the inhabitants of the Irrawaddy valley.

Opposite below: The Depot Corporals, May 1932. From left to right, back row: Cpl Cardiff, L/Cpl Brigstock, L/Cpl Lang, L/Cpl T.T. Pearce, L/Cpl Holden, L/Cpl Roache, L/Cpl Bourner. Centre: Cpl Peter Derbyshire, L/Cpl Graham, Cpl Ball, Cpl Hogg, Cpl Smith, Cpl Sidlow. Seated: RSM W. Allen, Maj. B.G. Atkins DSO OBE MC, Capt. G.D. Cooper, Cpl Mansfield.

A full parade of the Depot in the 1930s. In December 1921, War Office approval had been given for the Depot to be known as Ladysmith Barracks in recognition of the siege in the Boer War, in which the 1st Battalion had played such an important part.

The Officers, Warrant Officers and Sergeants of the Depot, June 1932. From left to right, back row: Sergeants Stride, J. Bailey, Mulligan, Wright (AEC), Stridgeon DCM, J. Knight, S.M.J. Brazier, W.A. Walker, E. Everett, W.C. Thomas. Centre row: Sergeants Hinton (APTC), T. Smart, E.E. Seymour, Derwood, Lt W.J. Douglas, Lt J.M.T. Churchill, Sergeants T.A. Kelly, E. Finan, Wrenshaw. Seated: Capt. Lewis, CSM Marland, Capt. F. Britorous MC, RSM W. Allen, Maj. B.G. Atkins DSO OBE MC, Capt. G.D. Cooper, RQMS J. Yates, Capt. (QM) Smith, ORQMS CHC Wroe.

To mark the close ties between the City of Manchester and its regiment, it had been decided to present a set of silver drums to each regular battalion. On 17 July 1934, King George V, as Colonel-in-Chief of the regiment, accepted the drums presented to the 2nd Battalion. He is shown shaking hands with Lt-Col. R.H.R. Parminter DSO MC at the presentation in Albert Square.

Opposite below: Ladysmith Barracks – the Depot Mothers' Union outing to Blackpool in July 1933. From left to right, back row: Mesdames Hassall, Campbell, Sidlow, Elliott, Hosker, Hyde, Hogg, Batten and Everett. Centre: Mesdames Derbyshire, Metcalfe, Hinton, Crossley, Berry, Linforth, Ormrod, Feeney, Crossman, Scott and Brazier. Front row: Mesdames McCabe, Lainton, LePage, Knight, Allen, Egan, Yates, Thomas, Smart, Saunders, Frazer and Worcester.

Mrs Peter Derbyshire and a number of the other wives were later with their husbands in the 1st Battalion in Singapore when the Japanese invaded in 1941. She and her family, together with many others, were evacuated, via South Africa, at the last moment.

Alderman Walker, Deputy Lord Mayor of Manchester, visited the 1st Battalion in Jamaica on 9 October 1934 and handed over the set of silver drums which had been presented by the citizens of Manchester.

The 1st Battalion left Haifa in the troopship *Dilwara* on 25 September 1938, bound for Singapore. However, due to the international crisis over the German occupation of the Sudetenland, the battalion spent some time based in Cairo, Egypt, where they remained until the Munich Agreement was signed on 29 September. On 4 October the battalion re-embarked on the *Dilwara*, reaching Singapore on 20 October. The battalion was then based in Tanglin Barracks where, on 28 November, nineteen silver bugles were presented to the Corp of Drums, each named after a regimental battle honour and all subscribed by serving and retired officers of the regiment.

Regimental Sergeant-Major John Currie talking to Drum-Major Hand at a training camp in the Egyptian desert. On 18 August 1938, he was with a platoon detailed to picquet high ground near the village of Majd Al Kurum. Coming under heavy fire and in order to secure more effective fire, he mounted and manned a machine-gun on a truck. Whilst firing the gun, he was mortally wounded. His brother, Joseph, also served in the regiment and had been awarded the Distinguished Conduct Medal in the First World War.

In June 1938, whilst in Palestine, Lt Rex King-Clark led a squad of the 1st Battalion on special duty under the command of Capt. Wingate from GHQ. This was a Special Night Squad (SNS) to train and lead Jewish supernumerary police against Arab terrorists. Pictured is one of their specially armoured 15cwt trucks. King-Clark was awarded the Military Cross for his work with the SNS and, in the Second World War, commanded 2nd Manchesters in Burma. Orde Wingate won international recognition as Major-General and founder of the Chindits in the Second World War.

By the mid-1930s, the need for a chapel within Manchester Cathedral was a brave objective both within the regiment and its many friends in the local population. On 11 November 1936, the Derby Chapel was dedicated as the Regimental Chapel of the Manchester Regiment in the presence of a congregation of more than 2,000 people.

King George VI visited Manchester in 1938 and a Guard of Honour, commanded by Capt. Spencer, was provided by the 8th (Ardwick) Battalion.

In 1935 the War Office instructed all regimental depots to hold 'At Homes', in order to show the average civilian a little about the life of a soldier. This demonstration of physical training by recruits at Ladysmith Barracks was given in May 1935.

A fund was established in Oldham to purchase a set of nine silver drums in memory of those of the 10th Battalion who died in the war. The drums were engraved with 617 names and handed over to the battalion, on behalf of the citizens of Oldham, by Major-General Solly Flood. They are now held in the Oldham Civic Centre with other items of the 10th Battalion regimental silver.

7

THE SECOND WORLD WAR, 1939-1945

The granting of Battle Honours to a regiment for its services in war is of major importance in its history. During the Second World War, the Manchester Regiment was granted fifty battle honours to add to the existing eighty-eight honours. Of particular interest is the fact that the regiment was not awarded the battle honour 'Dunkirk', although the 2nd, 5th and 9th Battalions all laid claim to this. However, the honour was only awarded to those who actually fought as formed units at Dunkirk. This ruled out the regiment's claim, although all the Manchester units had fought hard in this rear-guard action to make the Dunkirk evacuation possible.

Similarly with the award of the honour 'Lower Maas'. In this battle, every company of the 1st Battalion was engaged continuously with 53rd (Welsh) Division in the battle for the town of s'Hertogenbosch. However, the capture of the town was not designated by the Battle Nomenclature Committee as a special engagement. Therefore 'Lower Maas' was the honour which embraced this particular battle.

Following the Japanese invasion and capture of Singapore, the 6th Territorial Battalion was reconstituted as a new 1st Battalion. Below are the honours awarded to each battalion. None are shown for the 5th Battalion which, although it fought in France with the British Expeditionary Force in 1940, spent the remainder of the war on defence duties within the UK.

1st Battalion
Singapore Island, Malaya 1941-42.

Reconstituted 1st Battalion
Caen, Esquay, Falaise, Nederrijn, Lower Maas, Venlo Pocket, Ourthe, Rhineland, Reichswald, Coch, Weeze, Rhine, Ibbenbüren, Aller, North-West Europe 1944-45.

2nd Battalion
Dyle, Withdrawal to Escaut, St Omer – La Bassee, North-West Europe 1940, North Arakan, Kohima, Pinwe, Schwebo, Myinmu Bridgehead, Irrawaddy, Burma 1944-45.

7th Battalion
Scheldt, Walcheren Causeway, Flushing, Roer, Weeze, Rhine, Ibbenburen, Dreierwalde, Bremen, North-West Europe 1944-45.

8th Battalion
Malta 1940 and Italy 1944.

9th Battalion
Defence of Arras, Ypres – Commines Canal, Gothic Line, Monte Gridolfo, Coriano, San Clemente, Cemmano Ridge, Montilgallo, Capture of Forli, Lamone Crossing, Defence of Lamone Bridgehead, Rimini Line, Montescudo, Desena, Italy 1944.

The 2nd Battalion officers following mobilisation at Aldershot, 7 September 1939. From left to right, back row: 2nd-Lt A.E. Holt, 2nd-Lt J.B.H. Keitley, Lt W.T. Wilkinson, 2nd-Lt WRM Moss, 2nd-Lt R. Dobson, 2nd-Lt R.K. Rose, Lt G. Paulson, Lt R.W. Hilton, 2nd-Lt D. Derham-Reid, Lt J.W. Ward, Lt J.P. Dewar. Middle row: 2nd-Lt J.D.M. Kirkness, Capt. C.J. Abbott, Lt J.M.T. Churchill, Capt. G.A. Tod, Lt C.K. Mott, Lt J.A.C. Fitch, Lt R. King-Clark MC, Lt G.W. Ham, Capt. H.D. Dook, Lt G.C. Marsh. Front row: Lt H.O. Brien, Capt. T.B.L. Churchill MC, Capt. G. Frampton, Major F.A. Levis, Lt-Col. A.W.U. Moore, Maj. F.G.W. Axworthy, Maj. H.E.M. Hickey, Capt. E.F. Woolsey, Capt. K.R.F. Black. John Fitch, as lieutenant-colonel, later commanded 3rd Battalion the Parachute Regiment and was killed inn action at Arnhem on 19 September 1944.

First line reinforcements for the 2nd Battalion, celebrating with local French children on Christmas Day, 1939.

The Canadian intake, 24 May 1939. From left to right, back row: R. Smith, W. O'Hanley, W. Whyte, D. Morrison, E. Falkenham, W. Bailey, R. Rutherford, N. Eisener, A. Hall, T. McCarthy, F. Lewis, L. Andrews, C. MacKeowan, B. Rogers, W. Lambeth. Middle row: F. McCarthy, T. Nolan, C. Anderson, J. Foster, P. Duffy, C. Cruikshanks, S. Plougue, J. Smith, R. MacKeowan, F. Hayden, D. Watson, F. Rampton, R. Eisener, A. Carver. Front row: R. Goodman, A. Smale, E. Vere Hollaway, H. Smith, N. Nelson, T. Goodshaw, G. Crouse, S. Barwick, S. Zinck, W. Delaney, H. Walker, C. Hook.

Some seventy-eight young Canadians, most from Halifax, Nova Scotia, who sailed to England at the beginning of the war, came to Ashton-under-Lyne and enlisted in the Manchester Regiment. Some were friends and relatives but the majority came through the influence of Colonel R.B. Willis DSO, an ex-officer of the regiment then living in Nova Scotia. He was able to arrange their passage to England and an introduction to the Manchester Regiment when they arrived. A few had earlier made the journey in 1938 but in 1939 arrangements were completed with Manchester Liners to provide working accommodation each week for groups of four men on ships visiting Halifax.

The enlistment books in the regimental archives show that groups of four Canadians regularly appeared at the Depot and were enlisted until, by May 1939, there were about sixty carrying out recruit training. The majority of these young men went on to serve with 2nd Manchesters in the British Expeditionary Force and continued to serve with the battalion in India and Burma. Two went to 1st Manchesters in Singapore. Later in the war, many transferred to the Canadian Army and at least two joined the Canadian SAS.

Opposite below: A 7th Battalion Vickers machine-gun team at St Pol, France on 25 November 1940 – an episode in the Phoney War.

In the early hours of 1 September 1939 came the order for the Territorial Army to mobilise. Calling-up notices were posted and the deluge of Territorials arrived on the 3rd. Overnight the 8th Battalion drill hall, which might under normal circumstances have had difficulty in accommodating a rifle company, found it accommodating some thirty-five officers and 850 other ranks. Additional accommodation was found in local churches and schools, and whole rows of private houses in Ardwick helped to take the strain. In their off-duty hours, the Territorials found that their uniform ensured free drinks all night at the local pub. Shown are the Warrant-Officers and Non-Commissioned Officers of the Ardwick Battalion, photographed in a friendly Ardwick backyard.

Sergeant George Derbyshire of the 5th Manchesters recorded the following in France 1940: 'We met long lines of refugees, travelling westwards in a confusion of carts, wagons, perambulators, cars, push-carts, anything on wheels that would hold some bedding and a few treasured possessions that could not be parted with.'

A helping hand from one of the Ardwicks in Malta, 1941.

Singapore 1941. The last major task allotted to the 1st Battalion was the construction of a gigantic anti-boat obstacle designed to prevent landing craft from getting close inshore.

The 1st Battalion had moved to Singapore in October 1938 and were the only Vickers Machine-gun unit on the island. Defence exercises were carried out in October 1941.

Following mobilisation, the 8th (Ardwick) Battalion joined the BEF in France as part of 127 Bde of 42 Division. After taking part in the Phoney War on the French/Belgium border, they were detached and sent to Malta in May 1940. Although armed with 3in-mortars and Lewis machine-guns, these were never fired in anger.

A Bren gun carrier of the 8th Battalion painted in Malta camouflage, designed to blend in with the many stone walls and buildings throughout the island, 1943.

A stitch in time. Private Brighouse of the 8th Battalion darning his socks in Angliara, Malta, on 15 August 1940.

Field Marshall Lord Gort bids farewell to the Ardwicks on their leaving Malta in August 1943. From left to right: Lt-Col. G.A. French, Capt. R.P. Cooke, Capt. A.D. Crompton, Capt. Philip Wilson, Capt. B. Daley. After the war, Philip Wilson commanded the Ardwick Battalion between 1953 and 1956.

Officers of the Regimental Depot and the 44th East Lancashire ATS Platoons, which were attached for training to the Manchester Regiment in Ashton-under-Lyne during the Second World War. They all wore the fleur-de-lys of the Manchester Regiment above their tunic pocket. In the early days, many were local girls who lived at home and attended the barracks daily, working a seven-day week. On Sundays there was little public transport and those girls living in Hyde had to walk to the barracks for first parade, which, it is recorded, they did in a gang and cheerfully.

His Majesty King George V, Queen Elizabeth, Princess Elizabeth and Princess Margaret with Lt-Col. Edward de Wilton Wills and the officers of the 5th Battalion when they formed the Royal Bodyguard at Balmoral in 1944.

Opposite below: The 8th Battalion left Malta for the Middle East on 31 August 1943. Training began in Syria, continuing in Palestine and Egypt in preparation for their next role in the forthcoming campaign in Italy. On 1 March 1944, the Ardwicks participated in the biggest manoeuvres they had ever taken part in – Exercise Crocodile – alongside thousands of British, Indian, Greek, Yugoslav and Arab Legion troops. The operation area extended from the southern end of the Jordan valley to the hills and defiles to the east and west of the plain.

Above: 4.2 mortars of D Company, 1st Battalion, in action at s'Hertogenbosch in October 1944.

Left: The 1st Battalion Signals Sergeant enjoying a little wine on the advance through France.

The 8th Battalion arrived in Italy during April 1944 and served there as part of the 10th Indian Division until the end of the war. They fought in the battles for the Gothic Line, their final action being the major assault on the village of San Pietro di Bagno. A battalion anti-tank gun is shown in position at Soci.

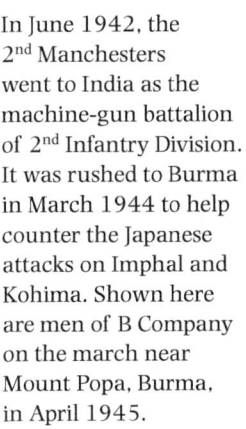

In June 1942, the 2nd Manchesters went to India as the machine-gun battalion of 2nd Infantry Division. It was rushed to Burma in March 1944 to help counter the Japanese attacks on Imphal and Kohima. Shown here are men of B Company on the march near Mount Popa, Burma, in April 1945.

It was across these 'hellish jungle mountains' of Kohima Ridge and the area beyond Naga village that the machine-gun platoons of 2nd Manchesters carried their Vickers and the heavy awkward tripods and equipment. One officer recorded in his diary, 'a tough magnificent body of men'. Occasionally it was possible to use Bren gun carriers and jeeps. Here a section is digging protective slit trenches during a short period of inactivity.

The 2nd Battalion Bren gun carrier team in Burma.

The 2ⁿᵈ Battalion transport moving below a bridge being rebuilt over a dried-up Burmese river-bed.

The 2ⁿᵈ Battalion mule transport moving along during the final stages of the journey to Mandalay. On 3 April 1945, a platoon of A Company took part in their final action before the end of the war. With two platoons of the Royal Scots, they set up a night ambush and wiped out over sixty of the enemy.

A Vickers machine-gunner of the 1st Battalion in action at the crossing of the River Weser on 12 April 1945.

After heavy fighting in the Reichswald Forest, Hamburg was entered by 1st Manchesters and, whilst there, the German Army surrendered. Pictured on 6 May 1945 are Lt-Col. 'Bill' Crozier with Major 'Archie' Tod on the right, leaning against a 'liberated' German Mercedes.

8

THE FINAL DAYS, 1946-1958

A patrol of B Company on a jungle path in the Bongsu, Perak State. On average, the struggle with dense undergrowth, barbed creepers and swamps limited patrolling to about eight miles each day. (Photograph by Ian Hanson)

With the reduction in size of the British Army at the end of the Second World War, instructions were received that the 2nd Battalion of the Manchester Regiment was to be one of many to be placed in 'token cadre form' and kept in being at regimental depots. It then became known that the 2nd Battalion had to either disband or amalgamate with the 1st Battalion and the decision was taken to amalgamate, this being the best way in which to preserve the traditions of both battalions and their predecessors, the old 63rd and 96th Regiments of Foot.

It was also resolved to add to the title of the new 1st Battalion the numerals 63rd/96th to signify the amalgamation. On 30 January 1948, the 'token cadre' of the 2nd Battalion moved to the Regimental Depot at its temporary home in Dunham Park, Altrincham, Cheshire. In May, amalgamation with the cadre of the 1st Battalion was completed and the 2nd Battalion Manchester Regiment ceased to exist.

Bren gun carriers from the Regimental Depot taking part in the London Victory Parade in 1946. In 1941, in order to save manpower, the Machine Gun Training Centre moved to the Depot of the Cheshire Regiment at The Dale, Chester, where it reformed as 24 MGTC. There it acted as a training centre for the four medium machine-gun regiments of the army – the Royal Northumberland Fusiliers, Cheshire Regiment, Middlesex Regiment and Manchester Regiment.

In November 1946 the Depot of the Manchesters was transferred to Dunham Park, Altrincham, which, during the war years, had housed German and Italian prisoners of war. Here the Depot, commanded by Maj. H.R.C. Green, became a joint unit with the 63rd Primary Training Centre, previously based at The Dale in Chester, and now commanded by Lt-Col. Philip Buchan. Training of recruits for the Manchesters and other Lancashire Regiments was carried out and the first recruits arrived during November/December 1946. The Depot officers were, from left to right, back row: Lt R.H. Bingham, Capt. E.E.J. Henderson, Lt E.M. Williams, Capt. George Towell, Lt J.E. Berry. Centre: Captains J.B.H. Barratt, A.J. Macdonald, John Teale, Capt. (QM) H.E. Newton, Lt F. Keeting. Seated: Capt Nigel K. Evans (Adjutant), Major H.R.C. Green, Lt-Col. Philip Buchan, Maj. Tim Goslin, Captain (QM) Herbert O'Brien.

Left: Her Majesty Queen Elizabeth, recently appointed Colonel-in-Chief of the Manchester Regiment, presents Col.-Sgt Jack Carney with his British Empire Medal at Dunham Park on 1 June 1948.

Below: The Queen meets the Old Comrades, Dunham Park Parade, 1 June 1948.

The Officers of the 1st Battalion at Wuppertal in the British Army of the Rhine in 1949. Standing, from left to right: Capt. J.A.P. McDonough (Border Regiment), Lt S. Woodward, Lt Robert Sadler, 2nd-Lt Robert A. Bonner, Lt Frank Buck, Lt John Adcock, Capt. Joe Walsh, Lt Arthur H.B. King, Lt John Stone (Canadian), 2nd-Lt Peter Smith, -?-, Lt D.E.F Jones, Lt Desmond Rook, Capt. H.L. Burden, 2nd-Lt Roy Parry. Seated: Padre Blunt, Capt. George Towell, Capt. L.W. Dickerson, Maj. Paul Rogers (Loyal Regiment), Maj. Archie Tod MC, Maj. J.R. Cole, Maj. H.R. Stewart (2i/c), Lt-Col. Charles Archdale, Capt. Robert G. Clutterbuck (Adjutant), Maj. George Frampton, Maj. 'Blossom' Almond, Maj. Martin Archdale, Maj. (QM) Herbert O'Brien, Capt. Peter McEachran, Capt. Robert Hargreaves (RAMC).

The Warrant Officers and Sergeant at Wuppertal in 1949. From left to right, seated: CMS Drake, Capt. H. O'Brien, CSM G. Osborne, Capt. R.G. Clutterbuck (Adjutant), Bandmaster Spooner, RSM Greenwood, Lt-Col. Charles Archdale, RQMS R. Jackson, CSM O'Brien, Maj. Stewart.

A representative detachment of the 8th (Ardwick) Battalion provided a Guard of Honour on the occasion of the visit of HRH Princess Margaret to Manchester on 27 March 1950. Lieutenant-Colonel Richard Martin-Bird escorted her through the ranks.

British, French and American forces stationed in Berlin took part in a combined training exercise held in the Grunewald on the outskirts of the city in September 1950. Here a Manchester Sergeant and American soldiers compare weapons.

Captain Bill Moss and CSM O'Brien on exercise in the Grunewald, Berlin.

The Lord Mayor of Manchester, Alderman Colonel Percy S. Dawson MM, visited the 1st Battalion in Berlin during September 1950 to present a Champion Company Banner on behalf of the City of Manchester. His photograph was taken with the Warrant Officers and Sergeants. Front row, from left to right: Bandmaster Spooner, RQMS R. Jackson, Maj. (QM) H. O'Brien, Maj. C.H.R. Hyde, Lt-Col. G. Frampton, the Lord Mayor, RSM A.E. Lomas, Councillor R.S. Harper, Maj. (QM) A.E. Handley, Philip Dingle (Town Clerk of Manchester), Capt. A.E. Holt (Adjutant).

Wavell Barracks, Berlin. The Adjutant, Capt. Robert Clutterbuck, accompanied by Lt Saunders, inspects the rifles of the B Company guard before leaving barracks for duty at Spandau Prison.

The band and drums of the 1st Battalion lead the new guard through Spandau to take over duties at the prison.

Above: Spandau Prison held leading members of the Nazi party found guilty of war crimes at the Nuremberg Trials. In addition to a multinational staff of prison warders, the four occupying nations each took it in turn to provide a military guard. Here Lt P.N. St J. Saunders and the Manchester guard, provided by B Company, take over duties from the American Army in May 1950.

Right: Regimental Sergeant-Major Alf Lomas casts his eye over the guard-mounting ceremony at Spandau. A superb soldier, he was described as 'completely impartial, always on duty, with nothing and nobody being missed by his eagle eye'. Later promoted Major, after retirement he became the Assistant Regimental Secretary based in Manchester.

Support Company marches past at the Queen's birthday parade, Berlin, 1950.

Wavell Barracks, Berlin, 1950. From left to right: Lt-Col. George Frampton, Maj. Bill Potter, British Police Officer, CSM 'Jock' Hill, Maj. Robert Edwards.

Albert Square, Manchester, 11 May 1951. The Lord Mayor-Alderman Col. Percy S. Dawson MM, inspects the battalion. From left to right: Maj. W.R. Potter MBE commanding B Company, Lieutenant R.A. Bonner, CSM H. Emmott. Colonel Dawson had been awarded the Military Medal whilst serving as L/Cpl in the 16th Battalion at Montauban in 1915. He was later commissioned in the 8th (Ardwick) Battalion and commanded it between 1932 and 1938.

The 1st Manchesters executing their right to march through the city 'with bayonets fixed, drums beating and colours flying' on 11 May 1951, prior to leaving for Malaya.

The 1st Battalion, commanded by Lt-Col. 'Tommy' Woolsey DSO, sailed for Malaya in the troopship *Empire Halladale*, arriving at Singapore on 28 June 1951. Now in jungle-green uniforms, the battalion lines up at Selerang Barracks for a final battalion parade before moving up-country.

Drum-Major Derek Reilly and the silver drums lead 1st Manchesters to St Andrew's Cathedral in Singapore for a memorial service to the men of the regiment who lost their lives in action and in POW camps during the Japanese occupation of the Second World War.

The main body of the 1st Battalion travelled from Singapore to Penang in the Landing Ship Tank (LST) *Reginald Kerr*. Hot and uncomfortable! Lieutenant 'Sinbad' Hall, standing centre, surveys everyone getting ready for disembarkation whilst the band plays on 29 July 1951.

5 Platoon, B Company now established in their remote base in the hills at Kroh, Kedah, Malaya. From left to right, standing: Pte Ogg, Pte Hilton, Pte Pilkington, 2nd-Lt Crispin Worthington, Sgt John Mulcahey, Pte Martleton, Pte Garth, Pte Young, Pte Patterson, Pte Carlson, Pte Lomas. Sitting centre: Pte Holden, Pte Sheerin, Pte Humphries, Pte Vick, Pte Callen, Pte Rowe, Pte Morrison. Sitting front: Cpl Boardman, L/Cpl Selkirk, Cpl Murray, Cpl Walker and L/Cpl Mather. Kneeling: L/Cpl Brown.

A 3in-mortar team bombarding suspected terrorist locations in the Foothills Estate, Kulim, Kedah.

Opposite above: The end of a day's patrolling. Major H.T. Roberts (on the right) and his signaller trying to establish radio communication from their jungle patrol base in Central Perak. Successful communications depended on well-trained signallers being able to work on their own without technical supervision. They also had to be of good physique, having to carry their load for long periods over difficult country.

Opposite below: Second Lieutenant John Penny of B Company, deep in thought during a break in patrolling through the Pong Valley on the Siamese border, September 1951.

Left: Constantly on the alert! Patrols were armed with No.5 rifles, Owen Guns and usually one Bren gun carried by a strong member of the patrol. (Photograph by Ian Hanson)

Below: The 1st Battalion Warrant-Officers and Sergeants of HQ and SP Companies in 1953. From left to right, third row: Sgt Marshall, Sgt Blankley, Sgt Leach, Sgt Hughes (19), Sgt Baxter, Sgt Pulford, Sgt Graham (48), Sgt Graham (14), Sgt Widdowson. Middle row: Sgt Montgomery, Sgt Pellowe, Sgt Hughes (11), Sgt Rawlinson, Sgt Kennedy, SSI Bell (APTC), Sgt Fahey, Sgt Murphy, Sgt Sheppard, Sgt Hughes (54), Sgt Phillips (RAPC). Seated: Col.-Sgt Jones, CSM McGuire, RQMS Emmott, RSM Lomas, CSM Carney, ORQMS Aspinall, Col.-Sgt Massey.

The 1st Battalion Corp of Drums at Penang in January 1954. From left to right, back row: Drummers Conboye, Tyrer, Isherwood, Humphries, McAlroy and Marsden, L/Cpl Robinson, Drummers Bramwell and Wallwork. Centre row: Drummers McDonald, Wilkes, D. Bailey, Donaghue, Aspin, P. Bailey, Carey, L/Cpl Feighney, Drummer Greenhalgh. Front row: Drummers Hart and Hosie, Cpl Wharmby, RSM G. Osborne, Capt. A.W. Davis (Adjutant), Drum-Major J.W.G. Pulford, Drummers Artingstall, Hill and Taylor.

Never mind the leeches – swamps, rivers and wet paddy fields became a normal part of the daily patrolling scene.

The Motor Transport Company at Minden Barracks, Penang, 1952. Seated on the ground: Pte Whitehead, Cfn Armitage, Pte Jones H, Pte Laidler, Pte Higson, Pte Potter. First row: Pte Downey, L/Cpl; Blankley, Cpl Glynn, Cpl Sugden, Cpl Minghella, Cpl Cheeseman, Sgt Baldwin, Lt Chatterton, Sgt O. Taylor, Cpl Blundell, Cpl Sale, Cpl Watson, Cpl Jarvis, L/Cpl Burgess, L/Cpl Whittaker, Pte Carruthers. Second row: Pte Gillibrand, Pte Bee, Pte Vickery, Cfn Kenny, Pte Holland, Pte Lavelle, Pte W. Wright, Pte Wilcock, Pte Kelly, Pte Whittle, Pte Todd, Pte Latham, Pte Storr, Pte Murray, Pte Parkinson, Pte Martin, Pte Johnson, Pte Beattie, Pte Cartledge. Third row: Pte Webster, Pte Normanton, Pte Readitt, Pte Blake, Pte Broadhurst, Pte Dawson, L/Cpl McKie, Cpl Parkins, L/Cpl Selkirk, Pte Selby, Pte Johnson, Pte Rudge, Pte Comer, Pte Metcalf, Pte Gillam, Pte Duckworth. Rear row: Pte Hynes, Cfn Boyd, Cfn Topping, Pte Fryer, Cfn Imrie, Pte Fowles, Pte Sheffield, Pte Thomas, Pte Corbett, Pte Pollitt, Pte McKee, Pte Rankin, Pte Kinder, Pte Wood, Pte McNulty, Pte Birkett, Pte Gardner.

Bidor Airstrip near Tapah, Malaya, 1954. From left to right: OCPD, Lt-Col. Neville Close-Brooks, Capt. Derek Prescott, Army Liaison Officer, Army Auster Pilot, two Royal Navy pilots.

General Sir Gerald Templar, High Commissioner of Malaya, came to bid farewell to the battalion after its three years fighting communist terrorists in the jungles of north Malaya. Here he shakes hands with 2nd-Lt MP Reid at Kuala Lumpur Station as the battalion leaves for the UK.

Happy to be safely back in the UK, Southampton, 25 May 1954. The 1st Battalion moved to Formby on the Lancashire coast before later transferring back to Berlin.

In 1949, to the joy of everyone in the regiment, the Depot was re-established at Ladysmith Barracks, where it continued to act as the headquarters and training unit for both regular army recruits and the new influx of national service soldiers. Brigadier Tom Churchill inspects the young soldiers at their passing-out parade.

Ladysmith Barracks in Ashton-under-Lyne had been the headquarters and Depot of the regiment since 1881. Standing in the entrance on the occasion of a 'families' day' are RSM Lomas, WOII Carney and Sgt Campbell of the permanent staff. Following amalgamation of the Manchester Regiment with the King's Regiment in 1958, the barracks were permanently closed and later demolished.

Albert Square, Manchester, 12 July 1954. New colour belts were presented to the regiment by the City of Manchester. Brigadier T.B.L. Churchill, Colonel of the Regiment, assisted by RSM A.E. Lomas, places the new belts on the Ensigns – Lt R.G. Lee and 2nd-Lt A.J. Farrer.

Warrant-Officers and Sergeants of the 9th Battalion at annual camp at Castlemartin in 1954. Seated centre: Lt-Col. J. Robinson MC TD, RSM O'Brien, Capt. A.J. Adcock (Adjutant).

Presentation of Colours to the 1st Battalion by Queen Elizabeth the Queen Mother at Formby on 23 July 1954. Front row: Maj. L.W. Dickerson, Maj. W.R.M. Moss, Maj. J.A. Gardner, Maj. R.J. Griffiths, Maj. R. King-Clark, Brigadier T.B.L. Churchill, the Queen Mother, Lt-Col. N.B. Close-Brooks, Capt. A.W. Davis, Maj. B.W.R. Baker, Maj. J. Flynn, Maj. R.G. Clutterbuck, Maj. C.A. Simpson. Second row: 2nd-Lt N.D.R. Johnson, 2nd-Lt P. Hudson, 2nd-Lt I.G. Smith, Capt. D.M. Fletcher MC, Capt. M.G. Rhodes, Capt. R.P. Macdonald, Capt. P. McEachran, Capt. S.J. Hall, Capt. P.D. Adcock, 2nd-Lt Turnbull, 2nd-Lt D. Pile, 2nd-Lt MP Reid. Third row: 2nd-Lt G.H. Reid, 2nd-Lt I. Hanson, 2nd-Lt I. McCabe, 2nd-Lt G. Golden, 2nd-Lt R.J. Murray, 2nd-Lt D. Neville-Rolfe, 2nd-Lt L. Dutoy, 2nd-Lt D.A. Willey, 2nd-Lt J. Edwards, 2nd-Lt D.S. Morphed, 2nd-Lt R.T. Owen. The Colour Party: Lt R.G. Lee, 2nd-Lt M. Yemm, 2nd-Lt A. Cowan, 2nd-Lt A.J. Farrer.

The 1st Battalion formed up on a wet parade ground at Formby, Lancashire on the occasion of the presentation of the new Colours on 23 July 1954.

The 1st Battalion returns to Berlin and detrains at Spandau Station where Colours are marched into position. The Colour Ensigns are 2nd Lieutenants Michael Yemm and Alastair Cowan, followed by the Adjutant-Captain A.W. Davis.

Eyes right to the Commanding Officer as the 1st Battalion marches once again into Wavell Barracks, Spandau.

A concert by the regimental band outside the Town Hall, Spandau. Bandmaster Bentley had recently taken over from Bandmaster Spooner, who had been commissioned as Director of Music in the Canadian Army.

Inspection of the 1st Battalion by the Commander-in-Chief Rhine Army, Wavell Barracks, Berlin, 1955.

Members of the Depot permanent staff and recruits form the Bearer Party and Firing Party at the funeral of James Pitts VC in Blackburn in February 1956.

The final farewell to James Pitts VC. From left to right: Sgt Stephenson, Sgt John Redwood, Mrs Stones (niece), Maj. John Gunning (Depot Commander), Maj. (QM) Herbert O'Brien, Sgt George Taylor, Sgt R. (Dick) Cameron, Capt. Arthur King, Capt. Tony Davis.

The staff of the Regimental Depot, Ladysmith Barracks, Ashton-under-Lyne, 1954. From left to right, standing: Sergeants George Rawlinson, Millard, Pearce, Devine, Taylor, Middleton, Stephenson, Gwilliam (RAPC) and Cameron. Seated: Sgt Hull, WOII Jack Carney BEM, Maj. (QM) Herbert O'Brien MBE, Major John Gunning (Commanding), WOI Alf Lomas (Regimental Sergeant-Major), Capt. Robert Bonner (Adjutant), WOII Cahill (APTC), WOII Higgins and Col.-Sgt Pierce.

7th Battalion old comrades watch as Col. Sir Thomas Blatherwick hands the flag of the 7th Egyptian Army Battalion to Maj. John Gunning for safe-keeping in the museum. On the left is RSM Benson and on the right Lt-Col. Bill Usher.

British Army of the Rhine was in the front line of the Cold War. The 1st Battalion, based in Minden from 1956, 'wiped the board' in shooting, winning the Machine Gun Corps Cup, the Machine-Gun Fire Control Cup and the Rhine Army Shield. They also carried off the BAOR Officers Team match, the Warrant Officers and Sergeants Shield, Light Machine-Gun and Sub Machine-Gun trophies as well as 11 Brigade Rifle Meeting Shield and the 'Falling Plates' Trophy.

The 1st Battalion turns out to welcome Maj. Roy Baker MC and his victorious Rhine Army Shooting Champions back to Clifton Barracks in Minden.

In the shadow of Hermannsdenkmal in the Teutoburgerwald, a location well known to generations of post-war soldiers. Colour-Sergeant Ken Armitage and staff feed C Company with their midday meal. Second-Lieutenant Colin Denning, wearing cap, is on the left.

A ceremonial parade was held at Brentwood on 22 April 1958 to commemorate the 200th anniversary of the raising of the 63rd Regiment in 1758. Sergeant Pepper, Lt Colin Denning and Sgt Brown troop the Queen's Colour through the ranks of the battalion.

Right: 'Nippy' Gannon, the Officers' Mess Silverman, at work in Brentwood, April 1958.

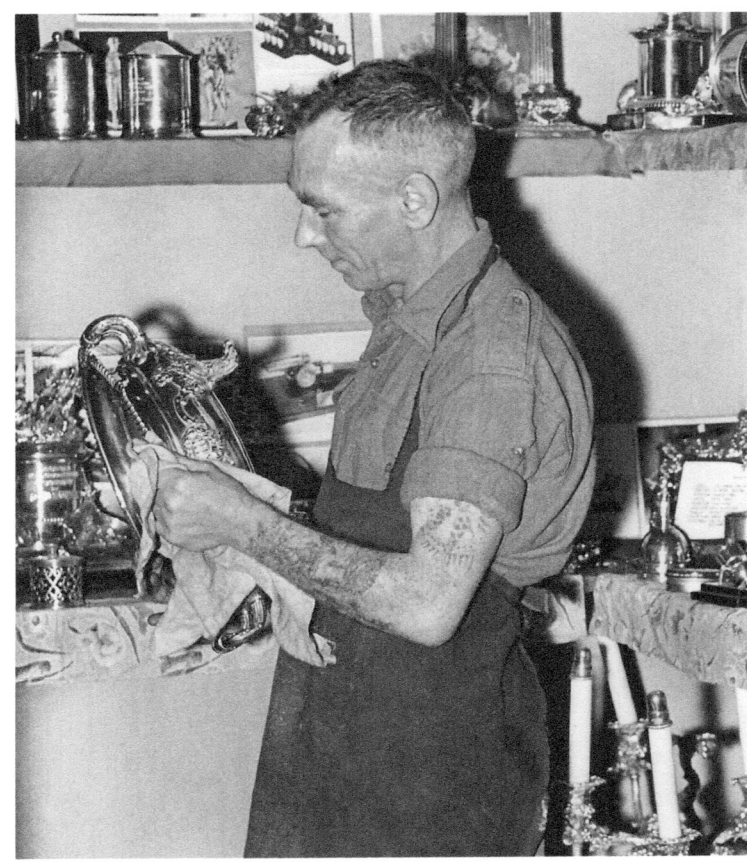

Below: Members of the Anti-Tank Platoon in training at Brentwood on 22 April 1958.

Left: Following the end of the bi-centenary parade, Regimental Sergeant-Major Harold Bellis presents Bandmaster Bentley to the Colonel-in-Chief, Queen Elizabeth the Queen Mother.

Below: Captain John Adcock, Lt-Col. Jack Fouracre and Capt. Tony Davis watch as Queen Elizabeth the Queen Mother speaks with CSM John McCabe on 22 April 1958.

Brentwood – the final days of the Manchester Regiment. Pictured are Lieutenant-Colonel Jack Fouracre, the last Commanding Officer, and his Adjutant Captain Arthur King.

Other titles published by The History Press

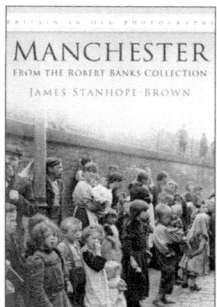

Manchester: From the Robert Banks Collection
JAMES STANHOPE-BROWN

This collection of archive photographs, taken by professional photographer Robert Banks working in Manchester during the 1900s, offers a rare glimpse of some of the events that were taking place in the city at the time. Featuring snapshots of street scenes, whit walks, temperance marches, football matches and royal visits, this absorbing book captures Manchester at the turn of the last century and is an essential volume for lovers of photography and everyone with an interest in the history of the city.

978 0 7524 6013 0

The Man City Miscellany
DAVID CLAYTON

The Man City Miscellany is packed with lists, statistics, tables, song lyrics, quotes and facts – such as the name of Clive Allen's dog, and the meaning behind the 'Invisible Man' the City fans sing about. From club record holders to bizarre goal celebrations, and from peculiar player nicknames to the ups and downs of City's chequered history, this is the only trivia book a Blues fan could ever need.

978 0 7509 4834 0

Greater Manchester Murders
ALAN HAYHURST

This book details some of the most notorious murders in the history of Greater Manchester. They include the case of notorious cat burglar Charlie Peace, who killed 20-year-old PC Nicholas Cook, and only confessed when he had already been sentenced to death for another murder; William Robert Taylor, whose young daughter was killed in a boiler explosion and who later murdered a bailiff as well as his three remaining children; and John Jackson, who escaped from Strangeways Gaol by killing a prison warder.

978 0 7509 5091 6

The Golden Years of Manchester Picture Houses
DEREK J. SOUTHALL

This is a delightful collection of memories from the golden age of cinema in Manchester. Filled with archive images, it recalls courting days and war-time air raids, the stars, the staff and all the magic of the silver screen. 'When my husband and I were courting, we used to go to the Rivoli cinema in Gorton. It was a very big old cinema, and we soon learned that it was advisable to keep your feet up on the seat in front. It was not unusual, if you kept your feet on the floor, for "things" to run over your feet.'

978 0 7524 4981 4

Visit our website and discover thousands of other History Press books.
www.thehistorypress.co.uk